in transit

in transit
josep lluís
mateo

Original edition: *En tránsito*, published by Puente editores, Barcelona, 2023

Editor: Moisés Puente
Graphic design: RafamateoStudio
Coordination: Cristina Marcos
Translation and proofreading: George Hutton
Print: agpograf impressors, Barcelona

Published by
Verlag der Buchhandlung Walther und Franz König
Ehrenstrasse 4
D-50672 Köln
verlag@buchhandlung-walther-koenig.de

Printed in Spain
ISBN: 978-3-7533-0559-2

Distribution

Germany, Austria and Switzerland
Buchhandlung Walther König, Cologne
Tel. +49 (0) 221 / 20 59 6-53
Fax +49 (0) 221 / 20 59 6-60
verlag@buchhandlung-walther-koenig.de

Distribution outside the United States and Canada, Germany, Austria and Switzerland
Thames & Hudson Ltd., London
www.thamesandhudson.com

United States and Canada
D.A.P. / Distributed Art Publishers, Inc., New York
www.artbook.com

FSC
www.fsc.org
MIX
Paper | Supporting responsible forestry
FSC® C104592

contents

6   **in transit**

8   **earth + sky**
a conversation between Josep Lluís Mateo and Juhani Pallasmaa

12   **housing in Heerhugowaard**
14   craftsmanship and prefabrication
20   architectural detail

22   **photography and architecture**
silence, darkness
texts by Toni Catany and Josep Lluís Mateo

24   **Toni Catany international photography centre**
28   a work in progress
50   photographing the Toni Catany international photography centre
texts by Aldo Amoretti and Gabriel Ramon

52   **telluric presence**

54   **central axis of the Grand Arénas multimodal hub**
62   under the paving stones, coolness

66   **school for the applied arts (ESMA)**
70   the first stone

84   **space, immateriality, detail**
86   Banc de Sabadell Space: interaction: front and back (city-nature)
94   Banco de Sabadell Welcome Hub: penetration (inwards)
100   Fundació Banc de Sabadell: space and encounters

106   **globalisation: a new phase**
a conversation between Xiao Lu, Cristina Marcos, Josep Lluís Mateo, Kevin Sun and Ren Tian

110   **project credits**
111   **image credits**

in transit

Montpellier, 21 March 2019

Josep Lluís Mateo. Architect, graduate of the Barcelona School of Architecture (ETSAB), Doctor of Architecture *cum laude* (1994) of the Polytechnic University of Catalonia (UPC) and Emeritus Professor of the ETH, Zurich.

Mateo was formerly Director of the architectural journal *Quaderns d'Arquitectura i Urbanisme* (1981-90).

His work, which encompasses a broad range of typologies — from offices to housing, as well as work in the public space and urban design — has garnered numerous awards, and has been published and exhibited extensively.

Recent accolades:

In 2019, the magazine *Domus* named his studio as one of the top 100 in the world. In 2022, his book *Footprints* (Park Books, Zurich, 2020) won the Juanzong Archive prize (China) for "Author of the Year".

https://mateo-arquitectura.com

Our recent past has been defined by the pandemic — lockdown, isolation, distance, immobility — and this turn of events has clearly influenced architecture: there is renewed demand for a more direct link with the outside, more proximity and more contact.

Some of the issues relating to that experience have marked our present, and they might well shape our future too:

The digital world is being prioritised over the material world, in terms of possibilities for meeting and contact. This shift is somewhat tricky to apply exclusively to our discipline, since although architecture is clearly rooted in the world of ideas and abstraction, its ultimate aim is to construct in the physical, material, real world; it's about how space and form relate to our senses.

Also, certain matters have now taken on greater importance: the connection with the outside, **the necessary presence of nature for human life, the active and positive relationship with the natural world.** As a result, today's debate about the city space — which was previously regarded in terms of its mere dense artificiality — has now become a discussion (and, necessarily, a broader project) about sustainability and ecological autonomy.

Until recently, globalisation was considered as a setting for infinite, limitless and non-specified movements. However, **it is now being remodelled, due to the emergence of new barriers and frontiers... today, there is a greater focus on the local, on the physical and cultural context.**

In my opinion, these changes are, in fact, in line with the tradition of architecture: the overriding aim of our profession is not to launch random objects into the void, but rather to find common ground in order to justify the specific proposal, whatever the architect's particular style might be.

Here, we have compiled our buildings and projects of this period (2020-23), along with discussion of the circumstances around them. This is more than a presentation of the results: we also reflect on the unexpected occurrences that affected (or even, sometimes, explained) the work and the moment.

This book features certain fragments of all those matters which, in turn, broaden our horizons and invigorate our work.

Josep Lluís Mateo, 2023

earth + sky

a conversation between
Josep Lluís Mateo and Juhani Pallasmaa

I met Juhani Pallasmaa in mid-March 2020, just as a new term was beginning at the Barcelona School of Architecture (ETSAB). He was due to be the visiting professor that term, a post that I had held the term before. We went for lunch in a restaurant up in the mountains, with views of Barcelona in the spring sunshine. However, just a few hours later, our whole world collapsed: we (everybody) had to lock ourselves up at home. During this long lockdown period, Juhani and I had various interactions and debates on Zoom, some excerpts of which are presented here.

Juhani Pallasmaa. Architect and professor. Pallasmaa has been actively working as an architect since the 1960s, alongside his theoretical and academic work: this includes exhibition design, as well as over three hundred essays and sixty published books. He holds honorary doctorates from the University of the Arts, Helsinki (1993), the Estonian Academy of Arts (2004) and the Helsinki University of Technology (1998).

8

Josep Lluís Mateo [JLLM] In our studio, we (you too, I think) understand architecture as a production of reality, of materiality. You were one of the first to talk about architecture's connection to the body, to the senses, in a way that described it as a physical fact. To a certain extent, your argument challenged the perception of architecture as something more intellectual, as an abstract idea, a notion. You've been a practicing architect as well, and, importantly, you've dealt with materiality. It's the basis of our job.

Juhani Pallasmaa [JP] Architecture, as with all the arts, exists in the experiential world; it's about sensory and bodily experiences. These kinds of abilities and skills have to be developed from the very beginning. For instance, students who use computers early on in their design don't seem to have any sense of scale, because the computer presents a scaleless image. I think there are certain problems that need to be addressed, somehow, within architectural education.

JLLM I think that perhaps, today, "architecture-as-reality" (the production of something real) is becoming ever more crucial: given the rise of the digital (that is, this particular kind of abstraction and virtuality), the real-world presence of things is now increasingly rare, but it's also more valuable as a result. It's like interpersonal contact: simply being with people is more difficult now, but it's also more vital and more exciting than ever.

When you build something, you produce a "first time", a first encounter with the ground. When you're there on site, you come across pieces, sometimes even archaeological fragments. Making contact with the ground is not just a metaphor; there are stones, different layers…

JP This is also linked to our senses. I've come to the conclusion that the most important sense in architecture is our existential sense. It's not one of the five individual senses: it's the overall sense of being.

Contemporary architecture has abstracted the ground into horizontality, but the earth is not just horizontality: it's also fertility, a deep memory, with archaeological fragments embedded within it, as you said. The notion of excavation has become highly important. Creative work is usually compared with exploration, but I think it's more like excavation: digging into something forgotten. Furthermore, if we think about housing, we realise that all houses and buildings have this connection with the land, and also with the sky.

When we think of the word *earth*, we can even smell it in our noses. If we speak about *horizontality*, though, nothing comes to mind. I think that's the problem with architecture today: it's so far removed from basic sensory meaning. Contemporary architecture tends to cut itself off from this fundamental poetic and experiential aspect.

JLLM The sky is another very exciting element for our buildings, because it enters into a kind of dialogue with the earth. I always think of Icarus and Dedalus. Dedalus was the father, who built all the walls of the labyrinth (connected to the earth), while his son, Icarus, tried to fly. We know that their story doesn't have a happy ending, but I think, for architects, this dialectic is thrilling, and very close to us. We are bound to the earth, but we try to fly.

JP Yes! The dream of flying is fundamental to the human mind.

One of the reasons why Jørn Utzon's best works have such a profound effect on us is because they celebrate the imagination of flying, like the Sydney Opera House or the Bagsværd Church. Both of these buildings draw our attention upwards, towards the air, towards flight.

I have thought and written about the correlation between questions and answers. I am of the opinion that in design, or creative work in general, it is not a matter of asking questions and then just answering them. The question and the answer arise at the same time.

Existential propositions are a combination of question and answer; they contain both parts. That's the nature of existence: it's always a question.

I cannot stand the use of the word *solutions* in relation to architecture. In Finnish, buildings are often referred to as solutions. Solutions to what, exactly? I don't think architectural projects are solutions. They are existential propositions. A mathematical equation can have a solution.

JLLM And design, a project, not only answers a given question, but also proposes new questions (or modifies the initial one).

This year has been, for all of us, a time for staying at home. Not many of our houses were designed for that, though.

JP I understand the home and the house as actions, as verbs rather than things. For me, inhabiting is a very broad notion. In the Heideggerian sense, we don't just inhabit our house, we inhabit the world. Architecture's task is to mediate that fundamental relationship.

In *The Phenomenon of Men* (1955), Teilhard de Chardin — the French priest, scientist and philosopher — describes and defines the philosophical notion of the "Omega Point". From there, the world can be seen as a whole. I think it's a very touching definition. Our home should be this Omega Point. That's always my personal experience: when I'm on my way home after a long trip to the other side of the world, as I get ever closer, my world begins to take shape again.

As I see it, the problem in this pandemic era — and more generally, in the modern way of life — has been the weakening of a sense of presence. Instead of being present materially, things are increasingly represented in a secondary manner. The home should be a place where these primary fundamental associations and connections are made. You probably agree with me that most homes, or houses, have become mere aesthetic abstractions, a way to show off the designer's compositional skills. However, today, a more fundamental level of meaning is now at stake.

JLLM In terms of housing, the functionalist school was very useful, but at some point it stopped being so. Its relations and laws and ways of doing... These functionalist ideals seem to hail from an older time with different needs, and we now need another kind of approach, one which is not purely quantitative (surfaces, hygiene, legal issues, etc.). Almost all over the world (including here, of course), constructing houses is closely tied in with certain limitations that are, in some way, relics of the past.

JP I completely agree with you. As Louis I. Kahn said, the basic unit of architecture is the room. Modernity, however, has forgotten this somewhat: rooms have been turned into functionalised activities. There are no rooms anymore, just functionalised activities, like in the kitchen, the bedroom... in traditional houses, though, they were not strictly functionalised this way. All rooms could serve any purpose. I think the Coronavirus situation has proven that this over-functionalised home does not function very well when peculiar situations arise.

There is a belief, within our profession, that architects and artists can invent meaning. But meanings cannot be invented: they are present in human existence. Meaning is when something touches those built-in and mostly unconscious ways of understanding being in the world. So, although I very much believe in the power of beauty, I am critical of it when it becomes detached from its ground.

housing in Heerhugowaard

the Netherlands, 2020

Three separate buildings surround a large inner space. Within the patio is the car park, which is partly closed-off and covered in vegetation, providing a backdrop to the scenery. The buildings contain the houses. Although they are each different in terms of volume and ground plan, together they make up a single urban form, well-adapted to the place and its usage requirements. The resulting form is suited to the domestic character of the complex, and it aims to be qualitative, varied, crafted, multiple and human, while also seeking to avoid the abstract and dull rigidity of so many contemporary housing blocks.

The buildings are cladded in bricks (a material of great historical tradition in the Netherlands) of different textures and colours; each part is designed to be relatively autonomous and specific. Within an urban volume that is well attuned to the place, the complex's domestic quality is enhanced by the formal and visual fragmentation of the separate parts. Their small scale is embedded into the complex.

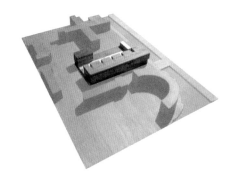

Different views of the external covering

craftsmanship and prefabrication

Working with matter is a mental activity, but any such task inevitably involves experiencing the physical, palpable presence of it too. In a paperless project, i.e. one built using digital tools, rationality, efficiency and prefabrication clearly play a vital role. The project here gladly embraced this newer approach, but other aspects of it reminded us of the ancient nature of construction: that is, the artisanal coming-together of hand and head as a possibility for sensate and material expression, in contact with the domestic life that these buildings are designed to host.

Trying out possible finishes with different types of brick

Prototype for the prefabricated wooden interior façades

Canal-facing façade (white brick, with large terraces)

18

Exterior façade: red and yellow bricks

architectural detail

Details of the brick joints.
Scale 1:5. Small sample.

Although the brickwork was extremely
artisanal, it still had to be designed and
arranged with great precision.

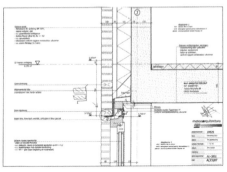
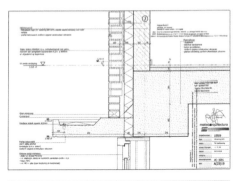
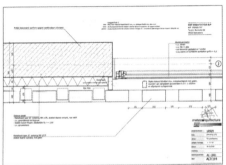
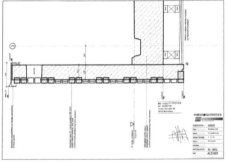
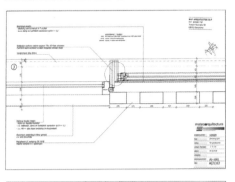
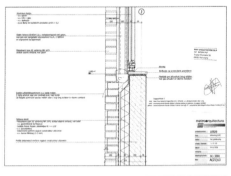
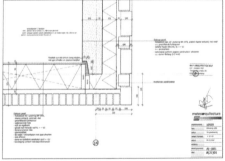
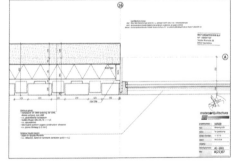

photography and architecture

silence

Silence cannot be heard. It is, perhaps, the muffled murmuring produced by the absence of sound in the ear. And, in that silence, the song of birds, of branches swaying in the wind, of dry leaves as they touch the ground, the rustle of some animal scurrying away, the lapping of the waves, the patter of our own footsteps.

There's also the silence of words unspoken. And the silence of the dead. Silence is the absence of sound, just as darkness is the absence of the image. Only in the desert does silence make sense.

El Silencio is the thought-provoking name of a ranch in the Venezuelan countryside, where livestock — cows, sheep and horses — graze beneath gigantic trees, such as saman and mahogany. It is also where most of the photographs in this book were taken.*

Toni Catany, 2012

* Garau, Antoni (ed.), *Toni Catany. El Silencio*, 2012, unpublished.

darkness

As I was looking over the pictures taken by Toni Catany at El Silencio, the ranch in Venezuela, and reading his text on the matter while listening to Frederic Mompou's *Silent Music* ("The silent music, the murmuring solitude", as John of the Cross wrote), I thought of a related subject, one directly linked to the photographer, which these photographs so candidly depict.

That subject is light. And, in the hands of the artist, its opposite: darkness, as the ultimate expression, by contrast, with lightness. Without darkness, without light, without shade, there can be no knowledge or perception of the physical world. Toni Catany's interest in darkness comes through in some of his work. As I survey these extraordinary photos, I pause at

two of them, which complement each other. The photograph on the opposite page has a certain tectonic, inorganic geometry, with materiality and texture, in which that hint of light brings depth and movement. It shows a harsh, rigid world, but one which is also dynamic and lively. The photograph on this page is organic, with a bipolar structure of clear-cut geometry: dark land, bright sky (enlivened by the roughness of the clouds). Above all, those sticks, with their irregularity, bring a certain vital chaos to the Cartesian order of the composition: they are desperately trying to stitch the land to the sky, using up all their energy in this battle.

Josep Lluís Mateo, 2020

Toni Catany international photography centre

Llucmajor, Mallorca, Spain, 2021-23

In the old town of Llucmajor, this international photography centre takes up part of the house where the photographer Toni Catany was born. The centre holds Catany's own collection, and it works to champion contemporary and international photography.

The place, the history, the remains, the scale, the classic house closed to the outside and open onto interior courtyards; all of these factors, clearly, form the basis for this project. It's about the phantoms or realities that stick with us, even if we should try to control them.

Nevertheless, we kept to our mission: to build a leading contemporary museum, suitable for showcasing exceptional works. We conserved some of the building's remains, rebuilding part of it, and we carefully restored the façades. The space is new, open, flexible, large, available, with very controlled light, sometimes even dark…

There are some unique elements too: a flying staircase, and a stairwell that recreates Catany's own world of colour. The protagonist, however, is always the space and the fine attention to detail, both radical and approachable.

From the outside, it looks like just another old house (the restauration was intense, but very archaic). Inside, it is a new and expansive world, where the works can truly shine.

We were interested in this duality: little village-type houses that have been radically transformed, without explicitly stating so.

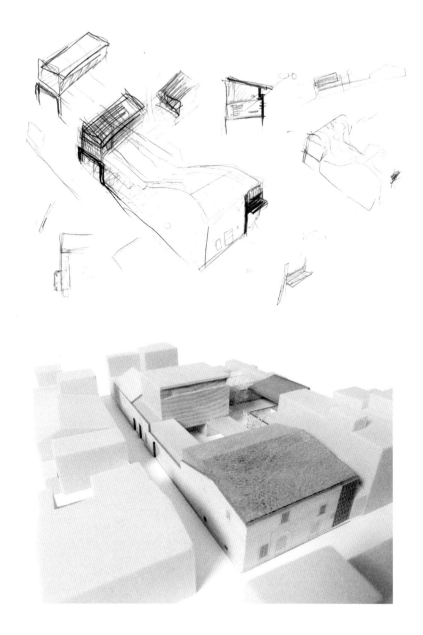

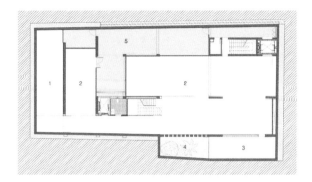

basement

1 Conference room
2 Exhibition room
3 Facilities
4 Patio
5 Storeroom

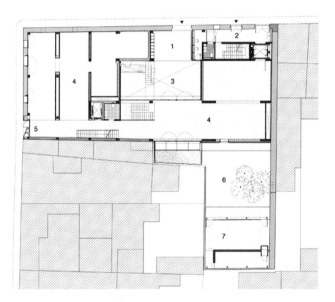

ground floor

1 Public entrance
2 Private and trade entrance
3 Patio
4 Exhibition room
5 Emergency exit
6 Patio
7 Educational pavilion

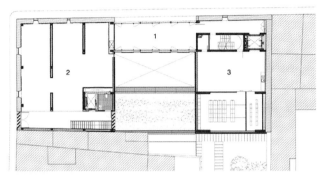

first floor

1 Library
2 Exhibition room
3 Restoration and negative store

second floor
1 Offices

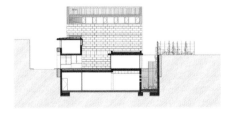

cross section

a work in progress

remains

25 November 2019

Beginnings. Clearing up. The remains of elements to be conserved, within a whole world of ruins, but without forgetting that our mission for the past is one that looks to the future.

4 August 2020

We dig. We extend the space downwards. We shore up. We save, and we will re-build. Earth, so much earth. Architecture begins (and ends) with earth, and it's omnipresent here.

detail

26 January 2021

Skywards. We raise up. We lift off the ground and start to float. We build.

23 June 2021

The finishes. Tough challenges to deal with. Sometimes with hope (though not always). Certain details — a handrail, for example — pose a real problem; it's hardly ever just a straightforward task.

Façade on Toni Catany Street

Corner where Toni Catany Street meets D'es Convent Street

Relationship between the old and the new

Façade onto D'es Convent Street

Main entrance

Entrance patio

Ground floor: main stairwell

Archaeological reconstruction of historical fragments

Old portrait. The house as backdrop, now reconstructed.

Photograph by Tomàs Montserrat, Mallorca's first photographer.

Exhibition spaces on the basement floor

Service staircase, with colours used in the work of Toni Catany

Floating staircase

First floor: sequence of walls
in the exhibition areas

Spatial interaction

photographing the Toni Catany international photography centre

It seems to me that there is a common thread between Josep Lluís Mateo's efforts to preserve the site's memory and the photographic work itself of Toni Catany: there exists a certain sense of stratification in the photographer's oeuvre.

Photographing the Toni Catany International Photography Centre was an opportunity for me to go back. I had the pleasure of rediscovering, re-examining, observing the work of Toni Catany (whom I knew), as well as looking back on his history and, therefore, the place where he was born and raised. I revisited his links with architecture, with light, with all the colour of the island of Mallorca.

As I went over his oeuvre again, I was particularly enthralled by his still-life photography; this is a timeless and profound body of work that remains incredibly current. I felt a kind of spark, which ignited within me an urge to try and capture that very idea of light… I wanted to get across that same timeless colour and light, so that the moment flowing within the photograph could come to the fore.

My objective, then, was to obtain that near-neutral light, without contrast and with low colour saturation. This way, I could be less subjective, less dramatic, less strident, and therefore leave open the possibility that the time embedded in the photographed object, its stratification, might even come to light.

Taking a step back, offering the architecture itself the chance to speak, much more softly, but still perceptible; almost as if it were telling me that the content of the picture was so strong that I could take a practically neutral photograph.

I enjoy working with Mateo because it's always surprising. He knows how to handle such disparate themes and places, but always with that clear, precise and recognisable voice of his.

Aldo Amoretti, 2021

Aldo Amoretti is an Italian photographer. He graduated from the Polytechnic University of Milan in 1992, and worked as an architect until 2005, at which point he embarked on a career as an independent architecture photographer. Amoretti has collaborated with many international studios and architects.

There was a striking amount of contrast in this project, because of its two priorities: to conserve some of the old part — it was impossible to conserve it all — and to build anew. The photography centre would safeguard the presence of Toni Catany and Tomàs Montserrat, who used to live in the building.

My initial photo essay didn't follow the usual script: it was more like a feature on an archaeological dig, where new elements kept being uncovered. I think the centre was designed in a similar way, somewhere between nostalgia and modernity.

My focus was to document the project, to monitor the construction site from the very start, right up to the finished building: empty at first, and later, fully functioning. I had no preconceived ideas. Photographing the Toni Catany International Photography Centre was a gradual act of discovery, with constant surprises, because I got to know the project, bit by bit, as the building work advanced.

For me, documenting something is all about seeking simplicity, retaining a certain logic in the work, avoiding visual effects of both perspective and colour. That way, those who go and see the building in real life can already feel a certain familiarity with it, because they've seen the photos beforehand. I try to remain faithful to the architect's work.

My approach is not about trying to explain everything in a single picture, because that way you end up saying nothing at all. Instead, I try to translate the immediate vision of it. Architecture photographers often use a large depth of field, but in doing so they risk betraying the reality, due to overemphasis. Authenticity should be what the human eye sees. My own viewpoint is that of the passer-by.

In practice, I do not see the definitive framing when I am taking photographs: 99% of my pictures are formed from two snapshots that encapsulate the movement of the eye from one side of the scene to the other, so as not to modify the perspective. I think that's how human sight works, like a telephoto lens in perpetual movement. I decide the limits of the frame, I more or less work out the balance, but I do not see the final image. I'll discover that afterwards, on the computer.

Gabriel Ramon, 2021

Gabriel Ramon is a French photographer, graduate in Hispanic Philology of the University of Lorraine (Nancy) and with studies in Photography at the University of Provence (Marsella). In 1980 he opened his studio in Palma de Mallorca, and he is currently working on black-and-white analogue portraiture, works of art for institutions and private clients, and architecture photography.

telluric presence

Text written for the exhibition *2020. Pamplona en casa* ("Pamplona at Home") by the photographer Pedro Pegenaute, held at the Palacio del Condestable, Pamplona, October-November 2021.

In the beautiful photograph of Pedro Pegenaute, taken in Pamplona during the lockdown period, we discern the solitude of the architecture, we see indoor light as an expression of life, at times a small human presence, emptiness, abandoned remains…

I stop and think about a different moment: the expression of nature's force and energy that freely spreads, over the silence, all around us. A sometimes-forgotten earthly presence, but which, here, is supremely present.

Josep Lluís Mateo, 2020

central axis of the Grand Arénas multimodal hub

Nice, France, 2020

This central transit route, which links the airport to the train station and the new bus terminal, features a tramline (that connects to the old town) and routes for other forms of public transport, as well as pedestrian pathways and lanes for light vehicles (such as bikes). This roadway is possible due to the new expansion towards the Val Valley. Different journeys, with different requirements.

1. The horizontal texture of all the paving has been standardised. The resulting surface is a continuous stone figure, set off by the kerb lines and some differences in size; the variation of the paving stones depends on what they are used for. The space between the tram rails is paved in rough cobblestones (to deter people from crossing there), while the pedestrian walkways have smooth granite tiles. The bus and cycle lanes are paved in high-strength concrete blocks. As a whole, these elements form a continuous, regular-but-varied tapestry.

2. The different parts join together in unique ways.

3. Plant life has been introduced into this mineral base: large trees line the pavements, the central reservation is green with vegetation, climbing plants go up the side walls, and there is a small park at the furthest point.

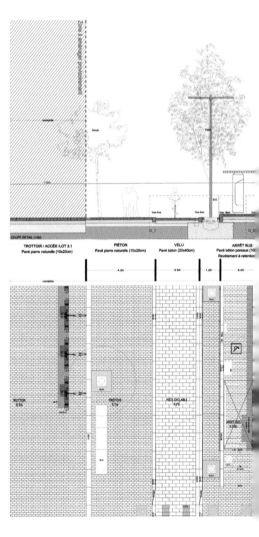

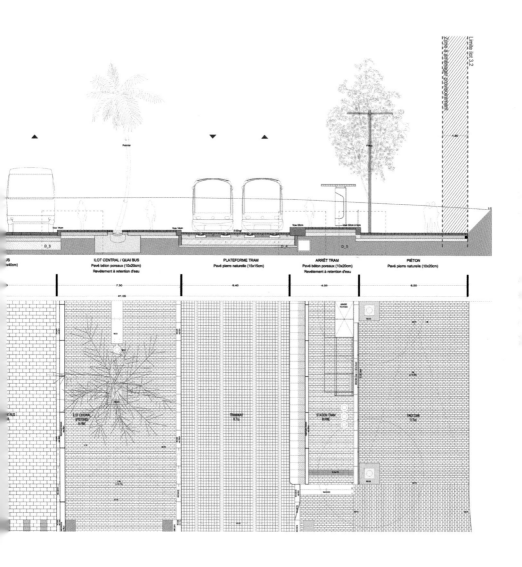

central axis of the Grand Arénas multimodal hub

Details of the joins between different surfaces. Textures

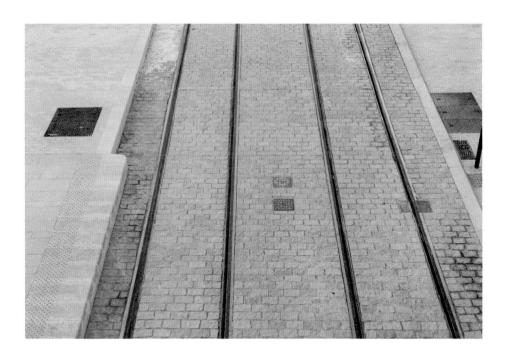

under the paving stones, coolness

Within the central axis of the multimodal transport hub in Nice, a large area of the road surface has built-in refrigeration, the first project of its kind in Europe. This technology has been incorporated in the areas with most footfall (bus stops, crossings, etc.), in an attempt to improve the thermal conditions in this increasingly hot climate.

This region has a high water table, so an underground irrigation system is controlled by exterior sensors that refrigerate special, breathable paving stones, made from mollusc shells.

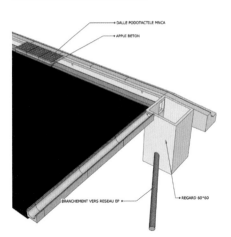

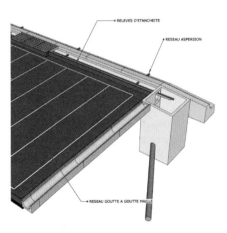

central axis of the Grand Arénas multimodal hub

central axis of the Grand Arénas multimodal hub

school for the applied arts (ESMA)

Montpellier, France, 2021

This school, which is dedicated to applied digital arts — special effects, animation, videogames, etc. — has an excellent reputation, and is now, in fact, spreading into other countries. The city of Montpellier is its base, and this building is its main operational hub.

ESMA is located on land that formerly belonged to the military, and many of the old buildings have been conserved. It has an inner courtyard (the former parade ground), although the building's volume is somewhat complex on the west side; there, it has new collective uses and allows sun into the patio.

The building has two parts. There are the spaces related to teaching — class-rooms, offices, canteens, sports halls, lecture halls and a large audiovisual recording studio — and then, above them, are the halls of residence, with a garden for getting around the site. This functional duality generates certain technical and spatial complexity. In fact, much like a mini-city, the building is a mixture of different spaces and diverse volumes.

The street-facing façades are more closed-off, for greater privacy. Those on the inside, though, which look over the (private) courtyard are more open, with larger windows, so they have sun protectors. The massiveness of it is tempered by the differing textures of the concrete façade, as we go up from the ground to

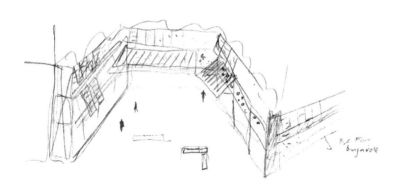

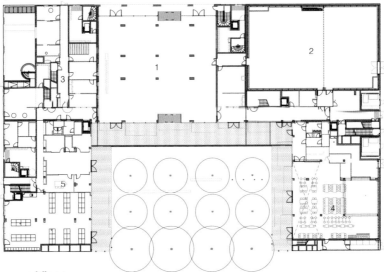

ground floor

1 Forum, public entrance hall
2 Film set
3 Offices
4 Restaurant
5 Spaces for academic use

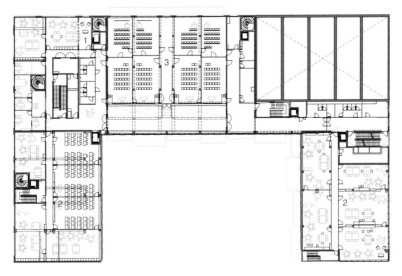

second floor

1 Admin and management
2 Classrooms
3 Lecture halls

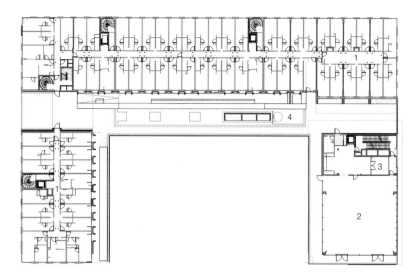

third floor

1 Student apartments
2 Gym
3 Changing rooms
4 Garden

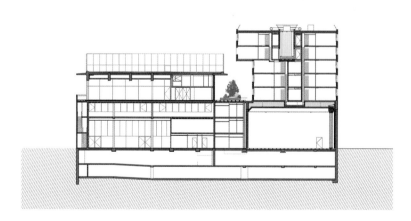

cross section

the first stone

The tradition of celebrating the start of the construction phase — the ceremony for the laying of the "first stone" — is a reminder that although our trade begins with ideas, these ideas must eventually become physical matter. Even if it's just a metaphor, the celebration is named after this first stone.

Ultimately, one of our job's fundamental moments is this encounter with matter.

Building has always been a collective operation. It requires the sum of multiple forces, abilities and energies, with a common objective. I'd like to acknowledge all those people who, with their hands and with their brains, have been involved in this process; I'd like to wish them all the very best and offer them my encouragement, and thank them for their efforts […].

We want this building to be more subtle than spectacular, more precise and vital than chaotic or spasmodic. We want it to be a building where matter is expressed carefully and sensitively, a place that one can freely approach with the gaze and with the hands.

We hope that this building, whilst it forms a good relationship with the existing remains of the old barracks (that is, the past), will be firmly oriented towards both the present day and the future.

Fragments of the architect's speech, delivered during the ceremony for the laying of the first stone, 22 March 2019.

Architect, proprietor and mayor during the ceremony for the laying of the first stone

The Montpellier Philharmonic Orchestra playing the soundtrack of a cartoon film produced at ESMA (at the ceremony for the laying of the first stone)

Audiovisual recording studio

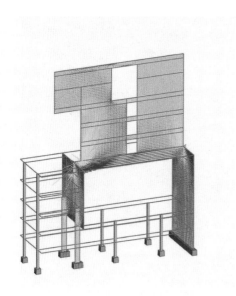

Transition between the smaller upper structure, with the living spaces, and the long-span recording space

Gymnasium on the upper floor

New transformation of the structure, to
prevent the need for columns in the gym

The structure's position has been moved, to generate the spacious atrium area (entrance hall and gathering space)

Indoor entrance hall

school for the applied arts (ESMA)

school for the applied arts (ESMA)   81

school for the applied arts (ESMA)   83

space, immateriality, detail

Defining space means working with emptiness, atmosphere, light, sound. Our reference points are always the usage, the movement, the place. Our activity constructs, metaphorically, the air.

This series of public workspaces for the new offices of Banco Sabadell really do aim to construct the void. In this context, though — which will be lived very close-up — the objective was also to build a sensorial and perhaps even tactile experience.
This explains the importance of the physical detail of our walls, of the material that defines the limits of the setting.

Building spaces is a beautiful mixture of extreme abstraction and distance, and, at the same time, sensuality, proximity and precision.

At a time when bank branches were undergoing widespread transformation, we created — as an experimental proposal — a space for both working and getting together. It would be open but active, as well as private when need be.

Banc de Sabadell Space

Madrid, Spain, 2020

interaction: front and back (city-nature)

Our intervention here seeks to enhance and dialogue with a preexisting space; it is not a matter of just slapping a perfunctory layer on top of the base. This is a central location, looking over the city and an incredible interior courtyard, with large trees and plant life; the dialogue with the exterior (that is, with the city and with nature) is the project's main aim.

While opening up to the outside, we hope to encourage interaction between the two external limits of the space: the street and the courtyard. Both are highly attractive, particularly the courtyard, which has many very leafy trees, like an inner-city forest.

When entering the complex from the street, we see a large photograph of the patio, by Jordi Bernadó, and it welcomes us into the space. This view soon becomes real, before our eyes, so these two distinct moments are brought into contact.

The language here is abstract, and great attention is paid to the environmental conditions (light, sound). This is a quiet space, with nuanced lighting and open yet well-controlled views.

Photograph by Jordi Bernadó of the block's interior garden

Entrance to the Banc de Sabadell Space. On the left is a reflection of the greenery from the street, while on the right we see a vinyl print of a photograph of the interior garden.

Work area in the entrance

Information point

The way inside: stone flooring, ceilings and vertical walls

Two-way transparency

First floor: private spaces

Banc de Sabadell Welcome Hub

Barcelona, Spain, 2023

penetration (inwards)

From the street, we penetrate deep inside. The space is arranged and formalised in line with this inward trajectory. Ceilings, walls and floors usher the motion through.

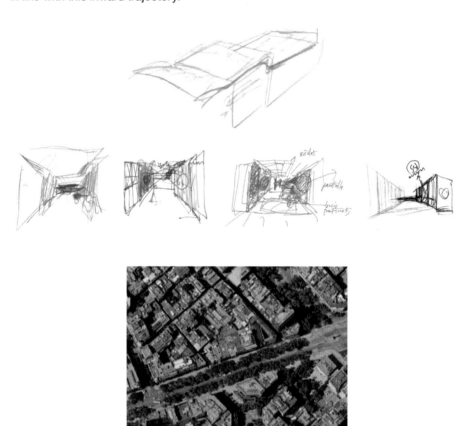

This space is organised across three floors: the central area, providing access and the image from the outside; the ground floor, a place for collective encounter; and the upper floor, a more private area for working and meeting.

Ground floor

space, immateriality, detail   97

Ground floor

Fundació Banc de Sabadell

Barcelona, Spain, 2023

space and encounters

The collective space follows the aperture of the large window that opens onto the exterior and submerges us right in the large crown of a nearby tree.

Small side-rooms accompany the flow of the space.

The space is organised around an open central area, with small rooms along its perimeter. The looming presence of a tree, opposite the façade, immerses us in plant life and acts as a kind of screen from the city.

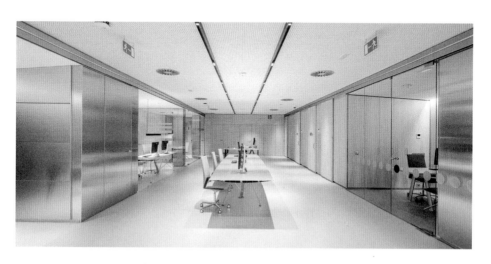

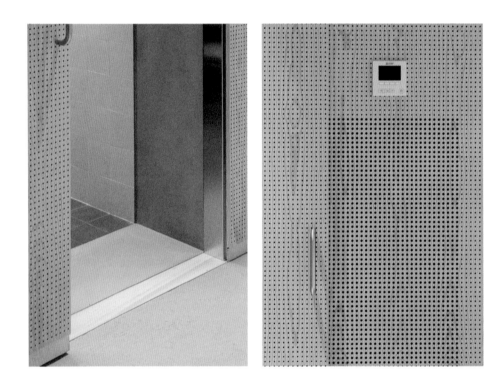

Encounters of different materials on the floors, walls and ceilings

globalisation: a new phase

a conversation between
Xiao Lu, Cristina Marcos, Josep Lluís Mateo, Kevin Sun and Ren Tian

In our contemporary world, where borders and frontiers are becoming ever more prevalent, globalisation now has a distinct presence. The world is increasingly heterogeneous, so any kind of infinite movement is no longer imaginable; instead, specificity and a local focus are regaining importance.

China is a paradigmatic case in this regard. During the early stages of its recent development, some decades ago, it seemed to be — as claimed by many critics — a new utopia for architectural and urban modernism. Evidently, it has not worked out like that; part of the country's historic heritage ended up getting destroyed, and the end results were nothing like the initial hopes for solid, qualitative progress. At most, this approach turned out to be the expression of a certain voraciousness, or sheer necessity.

This is a conversation with a group of young Chinese architects, all former pupils of the ETH, Zurich. The intention is to provide further details about the current situation of architecture in China, given its status as the prime example of globalisation as and when applied to our discipline.

Zurich, 2023

Xiao Lu. Born in Hangzhou, she studied Architecture at the University of New South Wales (Sydney) and at the ETH (Zurich), where she graduated with the project *7/24 Metropolitan Hybrid Machine* under the professorship of Adam Caruso in 2021. She is a member of the Swiss Society of Engineers and Architects.

Ren Tian. Doctor of Architecture, professor at the School of Architecture of the Central Academy of Fine Arts, China. He is the founder and head architect of Tian Ren Architects. He has studied at Harvard University, the National University of Singapore, the ETH (Zurich) and at the Central Academy of Fine Arts, China, where he completed a doctorate with Wang Shu.

Kevin Sun. Studied at the Suzhou University of Science and Technology, at the University of South Wales (Sydney) and at the ETH (Zurich). He is the co-author and editor of numerous publications, and has been the lead architect at deStudio since 2015. He is a senior consultant at Suzhou Kingting Construction and Decoration Engineering Co., Ltd.

Cristina Marcos. Studied Architecture at the Barcelona School of Architecture (ETSAB), and at the Tokyo University of the Arts (Geidai). She co-founded the studio Acto in 2020, and she combines her architecture work with independent research as well as theoretical, archival and editorial projects, in collaboration with other professionals and institutions.

Xiao Lu Two developments heralded the beginning of globalisation in China. The first was the rapid rise of modernisation and urbanisation, as a result of the country's economic reform in the late 1990s. The second was China's admission into the World Trade Organisation in 2001. China became the world's factory, but, because of overcapacity, the boom started to slow down after just ten years. Following industrialisation (the production of goods), it opted to produce culture, and rural areas were the ideal setting for this political demand. To ensure that tradition and local character would survive, but also as a way to revitalise tourism in these areas, a kind of "beautiful villages" slogan was created. These areas have thus become the places where young architects carry out their practice.

Ren Tian [RT] China's architecture scene has been always intertwined with the global, at least in some way. When Shanghai was a French Concession area, many European and American architects built western-style buildings there. In eastern cities near the sea, like Xiamen or Guangdong, immigrants from Southeast Asia brought their western-eastern style into China. Chinese people have always had this "bringing-back" mentality.

It was only after 1949 that the Communist People's Republic of China sought to instil a kind of national architectural language of its own. Liang Sicheng, who had studied in the United States, came back to help look for this distinctly Chinese identity.

Furthermore, and due to China's good relationship with the Soviet Union, the new buildings were strongly influenced by the Soviet style; architecture soon became a political representation.

In the 1980s, after Deng Xiaoping opened up China, a new conception of architecture emerged. A good example is the Xiangshan Hotel in Beijing, by the American architect I. M. Pei. It's a modern building, but at the same time it represents Chinese tradition (its ground plan is like that of a Chinese garden). Ever since then, the national style has moved on from being a large temple roof on top of a Soviet building.

In the 2000s, global "starchitects" built the centre of Beijing (Rem Koolhaas's CCTV Headquarters, the Bird's Nest stadium by Herzog & de Meuron and Ai Weiwei for the 2008 Olympics, etc.). This, in turn, issued a challenge to Chinese architects, who wanted their own starchitecture; Wang Shu, Liu Jiakun and Yung Ho Chang were part of that movement, and they still dominate the discourse. In China today, if there is a project to build a cultural centre or something, even in small cities, they will hold a large international competition. Western architects, however, need to find a way to present their proposals so that there is at least some cultural relation with the local.

Those of us in the younger generations still have many opportunities both in cities and villages, because there are a lot of works under construction. Many buildings need to be renovated: in the 1980s and 90s, the architecture was not built for quality, but rather quantity.

Kevin Sun [KS] In the 1980s, Chinese art had extensive contact with the international world, far more so than architecture. The construction of modern architecture has two facets: architecture is either conceived of as art, which can be traced back to the French *Beaux-Arts*, or as engineering, which may be influenced by the Bauhaus. There was no such thing as "Chinese architecture" before. We didn't even have a word for it, only words for buildings made by craftspeople (something closer to engineering). Architects saw how artists were becoming part of the global community, so they began to ask themselves: what can we do? In the late 1990s, architects like the previously mentioned Yung Ho Chang, Liu Jiakun and Wang Shu put on an exhibition called *Experimental Architecture* in Germany. That was the origin of what we now call Chinese architecture.

China's economy was booming in the 2000s, and I've always seen a parallel with the Arab Emirates: that same urge to possess a set of buildings that are ever taller, bigger and more striking, and designed by architects from all over the world.

RT If we look back at history, we realise that this cycle of closing and opening always comes back around. Before World War I, everything was very open: there were no borders between different countries, and people even had passports, so there was a lot of exchange going on. After the war, countries redrew their boundaries and borders. World War II, though, or maybe the Cold War, led to the need to cross borders. As a result, countries needed more exchange again.

Josep Lluís Mateo [JLLM] Covid had similar, widespread consequences in that regard. International borders were closed, so to cross them you had to fill in a lot of paperwork, justifying many things. I remember visiting building sites in other countries, and every work trip, usually such a straightforward activity, became an adventure of sorts. We were supposed to keep socially distanced, but our trade is very much based on craft: on building sites, where there are hundreds of people doing things, there is a lot of physical contact going on. Keeping away from others was almost impossible.

Cristina Marcos Following this conversation, I get the feeling that Chinese architecture is all about searching for a new identity. When the figure of the architect appears, the definition of architecture should come next: "If we now have architects, what do we understand as architecture?".

Architects share the strong influence of a (geographically delimited) "school" that establishes a certain tradition and encapsulates a particular way of seeing things. You've described a very clear moment of definition for what would be a modern Chinese school, one that still prevails, but which — paradoxically — emerged and was announced outside of China (at the German exhibition). So, how does that idea of a "school" relate to internationality? In another sense, when there are architecture competitions in China, even international proposals are required to interpret local values and take the context into account…

KS The issue is not about identity itself, but rather the fear of losing it. So, defining this identity becomes the problem. Some architects use formal references to ancient Chinese architecture; others, like Wang Shu, experiment with the materials used in old buildings. Some architects focus on ideas instead, and they use modern materials like steel or concrete, but they design spaces by means of itineraries and atmospheres, according to a certain culture. There are many ways to answer this question.

JLLM For me, architecture is not just some kind of object that turns up on the ground. With regards to projects, I've always be interested in relationships. When I start a project, I never know what I'm going to do. Some famous architects follow a kind of set pattern, so they invariably end up reproducing the same project, the same object. I'm more interested in the opposite. There are many factors that might shape the work, that can bring about certain conclusions and certain forms. One of them is the place, and not only in physical terms; every place has a certain poetry, a history...

RT To respond to the earlier question, when we work internationally, I do believe that there is a shared architectural language that we all understand. But architecture has many layers. Even though I believe that there is something very universal about it, there are things that are local. Our generation has had the chance to experience a global education, but we also have the opportunity to work in China. So, the culture, atmosphere and history strongly influence our designs, but we cannot deny that our education, experience or exposure to the West also has a bearing on every design decision. The role of the architect is not only that of being a designer: we are also negotiators, the intermediaries between many agents. We have to tie it all together, somehow. Often, the designing takes place on site.

JLLM I agree with what you're saying. We're right in the middle of a lot of tensions.

project credits

housing in Heerhugowaard
Location: Heerhugowaard, the Netherlands
Project: 2017-19
Construction period: 2019-20
Developer: Bouwbedrijf M. J. de Nijs en Zonen B. V.
Structure: Van Rossum
Electrical/mechanical installations and plumbing:
Hiensch
Construction: Nieman
Engineering: Koppes Bouwkunde
Surface: 8,500 m²

Toni Catany international photography centre
Location: Llucmajor, Mallorca, Spain
Project: 2018-19
Construction period: 2019-21 (opened in 2023)
Developers: Spanish Ministry of Culture, Government of the Balearic Islands and the Fundació
Toni Catany
Structure: BAC Engineering Consultancy Group
Facilities and sustainability: Deerns
Construction: Obras y Pavimentos MAN
Technical architect: Biel Garcies
Measuring and budget: Arrevolt
Surface: 1,200 m²

**central axis of the Grand Arénas
multimodal hub**
Location: Nice, France
Project: 2015
Construction: 2020
Developer: Etablissement Public d'Aménagement
de la Plaine du Var
Engineering: Egis
Landscaping: Atelier Villes et Paysages
Solutions for improved environmental quality:
Veolia-2EI
Surface: 21,200 m²

school for the applied arts (ESMA)
Location: Montpellier, France
Project: 2016-18
Construction period: 2018-22
Developer: Campus Créatif
Structure: BAC Engineering Consultancy Group
Facilities and sustainability: BET Durand
Planning, management and coordination of site:
ARTEBA
Surface: 22,200 m²

Banc de Sabadell Space
Location: Madrid, Spain
Project: 2019
Construction: 2020
Developer: Banc de Sabadell
Facilities: Tasvalor
Structures: BAC Engineering Group
Signage: Mario Eskenazi
Acoustics: Ivana Rossell
Furniture: Graó
Surface: 550 m²

Banc de Sabadell Welcome Hub
Location: Barcelona, Spain
Project: 2020-21
Construction: 2021
Developer: Banc de Sabadell
Facilities: ICA-Group
Acoustic consultant: Ivana Rossell
Measuring and budget: Aumedes DAP
Lighting: La Invisible
Sustainability and energy certification: Societat
Orgànica
Furniture: Graó
Surface: 950 m²

Fundació Banc de Sabadell
Location: Barcelona, Spain
Proyecto: 2021-23
Construction: 2023
Developer: Banc de Sabadell
Facilities: ICA-Group
Acoustic consultant: Ivana Rossell
Measuring and budget: Arrevolt
Lighting: La Invisible
Furniture: Graó
Surface: 260 m²

Mateo Arquitectura 2020-2023
Director: Josep Lluís Mateo; partner architect:
Patricia Klein; architects: Josefina Brizuela, Cristina Ferrés, María González, Till von Mackensen,
Cristina Marcos, Xavi Monclús, Arnau Pascual
and Pol Pensi; students: Alejandro Artigas, Adriano Cangemi, Xavi Granados and Iñigo Unceta-Barrenechea; office managers: Soraya Barbero,
Diana Guasch, Clara Matas and Sabine Willi;
communication: Lucía de la Rosa; model maker:
Enric Sanitja; economic control: Salvador Torroja.

image credits

All images belong to Mateo Arquitectura, with the exception of: pp. 6, 71 (lower), 72 (top), 73 (top and right), 74, 75, 76-77, 78-79, 80, 81 and 82: © Marie-Caroline Lucat; p. 13: © Jeroen Musch; pp. 16-17, 18, 19, 21, 31, 32 (lower), 33, 34, 35, 36, 37, 40, 41, 44 (left), 45 (left), 47 (top), 56, 57, 58-59, 60, 61, 63, 64-65 and 83: © Aldo Amoretti; pp. 22 and 23: © Toni Catany; pp. 28, 29, 30, 32 (top), 38 (top), 39, 42-43, 44 (right), 45 (right), 46-47 (lower) and 48-49: © Gabriel Ramon; p. 38 (lower): Tomàs Montserrat; pp. 52-53, 87 (lower), 88, 89, 90-91 and 92: © Pedro Pegenaute; p. 87 (top): © Jordi Bernadó; p. 93: © Dan Barreri; and pp. 85, 95, 96-97, 98-99, 101, 102, 103, 104 and 105: © Adrià Goula.